Jennifer Urezzio

A Little Book of Prayers

I0109092

A Good
STEWARD
Stirling, NJ

First Edition
First Printing, 2015

ISBN 0-9715678-6-7
13 digit ISBN 978-0-9715678-6-3

Edited by Mary Lou Stark
Design by Marty Marsh

A Good Steward LLC
P. O. Box 101
Stirling, NJ 07980

www.agoodsteward.net

Printing/manufacturing information for this book may be found on the last page.

A Note from Jennifer

A Little Book of Prayers was conceived at an event dedicated to love. Often we notice things about ourselves and file them away. I was noticing that clients and friends were asking me to write them a prayer to help them focus and transform their lives. I was noticing that I was writing a lot of prayers, and when I committed those to paper, magic began to happen.

Praying is a very personal act, and sometimes pain gets in the way and we are unable to find the words to express what we want the Divine to know. I created this little book for myself. I believe when two or more people set an intention, that force grows, and the words become law.

I suggest utilizing this book each day to keep connected to yourself and the Divine. For me, prayer isn't just for times of pain or struggle, it is to remind us of what is true. And to praise what is already true inside — and that which we wish to experience in our outer world.

With love and grace,

Jennifer

Acknowledgments

A while back, I noticed that my prayers were always about the same issues and that there must be a more powerful way of asking, accepting and claiming what I desire from the Divine.

My prayer structure is loosely based on the structure that Ernest Holmes suggests, and it is more about praising than pleading.

As always, no path and no prayer is created alone. I want to pause and acknowledge God and the following individuals...

My parents
Erin Saxton
Christine Clifton
Rev. Frankie Timmers
Warner Langlois
My Soul

For their assistance, I wish to show appreciation to...

Regina D'Alesio
Kathy Smyly Miller
Marty Marsh
Deb Cooperman
Mary Lou Stark
Alice Marie Braga

Table of Contents
A Little Book of Prayers

❧ 1 ❧

The Prayer of Everything

Everything today contributes and adds to my life purpose and my life force.

Everything today contributes to my manifestation of wealth and love.

I am willing and able to free connections that no longer serve me and my higher good. It is my intention and attention to connect with the Divine and be a counselor of Divine Love and Grace.

I set the intention and attention to be in the state of Grace in time and space for healing to take place and wisdom to grow and abundance and love to flow. My life is harmonious.

❧ 2 ☙

New Day Prayer

All around me is Divine Love. As the dawn breaks, so does any struggle and suffering within me. Today, the first steps I take are in deep love and gratitude.

Today, I remember how whole and complete I truly am. This is the consciousness I bring to every moment of my day. I step into the reality that I am an abundant being. I am willing and able to participate in those thoughts, feelings and activities that support this truth.

I am unafraid when conflicting thoughts come up. I allow them to pass through me, for today is a new conscious start.

I create and learn via joy and embrace this day for all it offers me.

⚜ 3 ⚜

Gratitude for Love

In this moment, I remember how deeply loved I am. This love fills my heart and any places of doubt in my body, my energy and my life.

My grateful heart lights my path, and it is what I remember right here.

I take a moment to thank all those who have touched my life. With a full heart of love and gratitude, I offer this back into the Universe, knowing it will return to me ten fold.

I know that I am safe to feel this love fully and completely.

❧ 4 ❧

Prayer for a Broken Heart

I know right now I am full of fear, pain and sorrow.

I know that Divine Love can ease this pain and sorrow
only after I have allowed myself to feel my feelings.

I know that I feel that I might be consumed by the
pain and sorrow of this broken heart. And right now
I wish to hear the Divine words that will ease the
pain in my heart.

I have a willingness to allow Divine Love into my
heart, not to avoid or hide from my feelings but to
allow the seed of hope, trust and love to be planted
again.

Knowing that this seed will continue to grow and
expand. That love is and will continue to bloom in my
heart. That this willingness to experience Divine Love
will allow the truth to be known, allow me to feel that
part of me that knows no wounds.

I am so grateful for this Divine seed in my heart and
even in my pain and sorrow, I know it is there, always
growing.

⇥ 5 ⇤

Letting Go of Fear

I know my mind is trying to take control of my truth, and with full love in my heart, I bless my mind. I allow myself to pause and feel the truth deep within my Soul, knowing that all is well and that I am safe.

I can feel the beginning of change that this knowing that I am safe creates in my life, starting right here and now.

I pause and remember a time when I moved through fear and on the other side felt blissful and bountiful.

Fear does not mean that I am doing anything wrong. In fact, it means that I am growing and expanding and my mind is reacting to keep me in an illusion of safety.

I do not have to fight or dissolve this fear. I do not have to do anything with this emotion, just allow it to pass through me and turn towards the truth of my Soul and Divine Truth.

I am always in a state of Divine Love and Grace. And, when the mind starts again, I once again pause and turn toward this truth – I am Divine Love and Grace.

⚜ 6 ⚜

A Prayer for Freedom

Today I connect to the freedom within me. I know that this freedom is within me because it is within the Divine and I am one with the Divine.

Even if that freedom is a little seed, I am aware of it, and I nurture it and feel it grow inside of me. This freedom helps me know the next Divinely inspired action to take that will generate more feelings of freedom.

This seed of freedom knows that I am safe and provided for and shows me the way to experience this truth in my outer world.

This freedom is my beacon, and it provides the love that will break those replicating patterns of bondage.

I am free, and today I express and embody this truth.

⇥ 7 ⇤

A Prayer of Connection

Some part of me knows that I am one with the Divine and that I am an unlimited being. And yet, I still feel separate.

Today, I am willing and able to know and experience the truth of my own Divinity.

Today, I am willing and able to let go of those situations, experiences and beliefs that keep me in the illusion of limitation.

All I need to do is be willing, and the Divine will handle the rest. My heart opens and is filled with gratitude as I step into this new connection with my unlimited Source.

⊰ 8 ⊱

A Prayer of Understanding

Today, I am tuned into my essential nature that knows the path to understanding and clarity.

Allowing and accepting that I am human and I might be afraid of what is next and yet, I can pause and allow my essential self to fill me with safety, and in doing so, understanding and clarity emerge.

I do not require all the answers. I am willing to understand and take the next step.

I am deeply grateful for myself in collaborating with my essential nature. I open up to the understanding that where I am is the moment of all creation.

❄ 9 ❄

Handing Over the Reins
to the Divine

Today, I acknowledge I am one with the Divine.

Today, I accept my power to collaborate with the Universe and Divine Love particles.

Today, I know I am Divine, and the Divine supports me.

Today, I walk in deep gratitude for my connection, for the love inside of me and for life.

Today, I allow God to be a part of my life, and I hand over the reins to the Divine.

In doing so, I am free.

❧ 10 ❧

Relationship with Money

Today, my relationship with money is Divine. Today, I know and experience Divine flow, and I am sustained financially with every move I make and with every choice.

I am living a life of ease and grace, love and abundance. I feel and experience safety and certainty with money.

I am full of trust and deeply grateful for Divine Love and support, which includes money, and I know that I am following my Divine Path. Every turn and choice I make invites the Divine into the equation.

I continue to choose to release all those thoughts and beliefs in conflict with the above truths.

I am grateful for this sustainable relationship with the Divine and money.

⇥11⇤

Lift the Struggle

Divine, today I seem to be struggling. Today, I seem to be filled with doubt. Today, my prayer is one of guiding me to turn towards what is true—that I am a Divine being.

Today, my intention is to witness more of the truth of my Divine being. Please fill me with a little more peace and a little more love, so that I may face this challenge with grace.

I accept that I am where I am and let go of wanting things to be different. In accepting where I am, I can choose to feel powerful. I can accept that this isn't happening to me but through me.

Somewhere in my being is the knowledge that this struggle will be lifted from my heart, and I pause to be grateful for that deep knowledge.

❧12❧

All Is Good

There is a creative force in the Universe, and this force is love. In this creative force, which I call the Divine, all is possible.

All is good, and all is well. I know and feel that I am a part of this creative force, so I know that within me are all possibilities. All is well, and all is good.

Today, I trust that all is good, and I am ready to experience the creative mind in action. I am willing and able to experience more of the good of the Universe.

I am grateful for this knowing, and I am grateful to the Source within me, and I open up and receive.

I can let go of the how and of control. I am willing and able for doubt and fear not to be the rulers of my world because in my world and in the Divine's world fear and doubt do not exist.

⇥13⇤

My Source Is Love

Source is all over and in every aspect of my life. The energy of Source is infinite and unstoppable love. Everything is feasible with Source. I am ready to experience more of the infinite possibilities.

I am ready to participate in a life full of support, patience, miracles and love. I am a part of the Infinite, and so what is true for this energy is inside of me. It is my resource and my Source of power.

To activate that unlimited power, I simply utter the word "trust." Today, everything and anything is feasible, and I am filled with joy knowing this to be true.

I am filled with awe at how love is showing up in my life and pause to be grateful for love in my life. I can let go of attachment and allow Source to be the love in my life.

⇥14⇤

I Am Creation

The Divine is in every moment of my life and in every action I take. I see and feel this presence in my life and within me.

I am one with creation. Today, I trust this creative force inside of me and step into the stream of love and abundance. Within me, peace is created, and this peace extends to my outer world.

I participate in my creation of peace and love, and gratitude fills my heart to let go and allow the Universe to support, hold and guide me in the creation process.

I create miracles today. I am the miracle today.

⇥15⇤

Unification of Love

With every breath, I can feel love within me. I can feel those parts that are in doubt and fear coming home to love again.

This unification of love reminds me that I am love, I am trust, I am abundance and I am grace.

I let this feeling of love and trust surround and support me. Love and trust are my guideposts on today's journey, and, with great relief, I hand over control to the Divine and relax in gratitude.

16

The Bigness of the Divine

Today with praise, I attempt to express the vastness and bigness of the Divine. Divine displays itself in every moment in time.

Today and each day, I know that I am Divine expression, that I too am a force of Universal Love and goodness. I declare that today I walk in the full expression of the Divine. I release all that does not resonate with this truth.

Today, knowing I am not alone, I walk in freedom. I am so grateful for my partner in this life—the Divine. I release all my doubts and fears to the Infinite.

The Divine will hold my dreams safe, help me to fulfill them and prepare me for my greatness.

All I need to do is accept and participate.

I accept that I am the bigness of the Divine.

⇥17⇤

I Am Present

Love is forever present. I am willing and able to be present to the love within me today. A surge of love flows through me, and the result is a life that reflects the love and freedom I feel inside.

Being present allows me to participate in the bounty of life, in the joy of life and in the profound experience of being human.

In the present, there is no judgment. Miracles are created in present time, and the Divine and I are miracle makers.

The past and the future have no hold over me because the present is where my energy is flowing.

I am ready to be present to the love that surrounds me and to the messages from the Divine.

⚜18⚜

Sweet Divine

Oh sweet Divine, full of love, full of grace. That bliss of love and support. I know I am one with you today. I can see and feel the expression of the oneness within me and around me.

The sweetness that is Divine Love fills every corner of my being. It washes away the pain and sorrow, and once again I know that I am powerful.

I am so grateful and can let go of all that is not in alignment with the One. I am ready and willing to express the sweetness of deep connection and the love of the Divine.

❧19❧

I Release Control
Over the How

There is a part of me aware that I am supported by
the Divine. Right here and right now I tune into that
part of me to guide and lead the way to my next
steps.

I accept that I am afraid or worried and still turn
towards that part of me that is invisible to the eye
and powerful. Today may present challenges, and
yet I know that miracles happen every moment of
every day.

Here I am ready and willing to hand over control to
the Divine and use my power of control to choose to
be supported. In letting go of how things will change
and trusting that they are transforming, I am free to
utilize my essential nature.

Ready to accept Divine Providence, I am safe to let
go of control and participate in how the Universe is
conspiring for me.

With a heart full of compassion and gratitude, I am
ready to co-create with the how of the Universe and
be profoundly supported by the Divine.

❦20❧

Renewed Health

I know that I am Divine. Within my Divinity is the abundance of health and vitality.

If I am experiencing challenges in my health, I allow the place in me that knows that I am unlimited to share this fact with my body so it can be renewed.

I can feel Soul running through my system and love repairing those parts of my DNA that are in distress. I can feel the life force flowing back into every part of my being.

I allow myself to step into safety with my body. I activate the love in my heart and offer this Divine Love to myself, my body and my life. As I offer this love, where there has been pain or distress, there is now only love and renewal.

I acknowledge that my body supports me and the Divine in me. Today I feel that support and Divinity pulsing and renewing my life.

About the Author

Jennifer Urezzio specializes in helping people connect—to themselves, to each other, and to the Divine. She founded a new paradigm, Soul Language, which provides insight into how the Soul expresses itself as being. The paradigm is embraced by top healers, lifestyle coaches and CEOs all over the world as a method for helping people recognize their purpose and live from a place of power and truth.

Jennifer was born and raised in New York. Her early career was in corporate America as a media relations specialist. In 2007, she decided to follow her Soul's calling and began showing people how to use Soul Language as a tangible tool to better understand who they are, develop their intuitive abilities, and heal through their own insight. Jennifer now lives in New Jersey and travels to meet with members of the Soul Language community. She speaks professionally and offers classes, workshops, and private consultations in person and by phone.

Her first book, *Soul Language: Consciously Connecting With Your Soul for Success,* was published in 2013 and has been embraced by individuals all over the world.

You can learn more about the book and Soul Language at www.soullanguage.us.

Jennifer is considered a master prayer writer and has been crafting prayers for her clients for years. If you wish to contact Jennifer and have her create a personal prayer for you she can be reached at:

jennifer@knowsoulslanguage.net

This collection is the one that Jennifer and her community turn to most for solace.